HOLIDAY CAMPS

Kathryn Ferry

SHIRE PUBLICATIONS

Published in Great Britain in 2011 by Shire Publications Ltd, Midland House, West Way, Botley, Oxford OX2 0PH, United Kingdom.
44-02 23rd Street, Suite 219, Long Island City, NY 11101, USA.

E-mail: shire@shirebooks.co.uk   www.shirebooks.co.uk

© 2010 Kathryn Ferry. First published 2010; reprinted 2011.

A CIP catalogue record for this book is available from the British Library.

Shire Library no. 591   •   ISBN-13: 978 0 74780 775 9

Kathryn Ferry has asserted her right under the Copyright, Designs and Patents Act, 1988, to be identified as the author of this book.

Designed by Tony Truscott Designs, Sussex, UK and typeset in Perpetua and Gill Sans.
Printed in China through Worldprint Ltd.

11 12 13 14 15   11 10 9 8 7 6 5 4 3 2

COVER IMAGE

Families enjoy the outdoor swimming pool at a Butlin's camp in the late 1950s. The company motto was borrowed from Shakespeare and announced in large red letters that read 'Our true intent is all for your delight'.

TITLE PAGE IMAGE

Song-sheet cover from the 1940s. The chorus runs: 'At a holiday camp one summer's day, Her tiny chalet was just next door but two, When she said "Hello" then my heart said "Oh, here's the girl for you".'

CONTENTS PAGE IMAGE

A 1950s cartoon reminder that camp spirit relied on co-operation and consideration.

ACKNOWLEDGEMENTS

My thanks to Roger Billington at Butlins Archive, Paul Smith at Thomas Cook Archives, Glen Fairweather, Carol Ryan, Janet Atkinson, Adrian, Sandra and James Baldwin, the Reverend Guy Bennett, Muriel Martin, Doreen Ferry, Wendy Bevan-Mogg, Mrs J. Townsend, Deborah Gohan at the North Devon Local Studies Library, Pamela Knight, David Gwynn, Tony Sharkey at Blackpool Library, Jenny Loveridge at Morecambe Library, Kim Haken at Rhyl Library, and all the librarians at Skegness. Last, but by no means least, I thank Matthew Slocombe and my parents, Michael and Vanessa.

All Butlins images are reproduced by kind permission of the Butlins Archive.

Other illustrations are acknowledged as follows:
Janet Atkinson, page 47 (top); James Alan Baldwin, pages 39 (top), and 43 (bottom right); the Reverend Guy Bennett, page 37 (top left); Wendy Bevan-Mogg, page 60 (bottom); Thomas Cook Archives, pages 12, 19 (bottom), 20, 28, and 31 (bottom); Glen Fairweather Collection, pages 21, 30, 35 (top), 39 (bottom), 43 (top), 50 (bottom), and 57 (middle); John Hinde, pages 33 and 53 (bottom); Jarrold & Sons Ltd., page 59 (bottom); R. L. Knight, page 10 (top and bottom); Muriel Martin, pages 38 (top), 44 (middle), 46 (top), and 51; NRM/Science & Society Picture Library, page 18; Carol Ryan, pages 29 (bottom), and 63; and Mrs J. Townsend, page 47 (bottom).

All other material is from the author's collection.

Shire Publications is supporting the Woodland Trust, the UK's leading woodland conservation charity, by funding the dedication of trees.

CONTENTS

COMMUNAL CAMPING

ATTITUDES to leisure changed hugely during the twentieth century. In 1938 the right to paid holidays became enshrined in law. For the millions of people now able to enjoy an annual break, holiday camps offered a welcome alternative to the inflexible rules of seaside landladies, the variable quality of boarding-house meals and the uncertain cost of promenade amusements. For a one-off, all-in price, the holiday camp provided accommodation, food *and* entertainment. In the 1930s this was nothing short of revolutionary.

Entrepreneurs such as Billy Butlin, Harry Warner and Fred Pontin are well-known for running chains of successful camps, yet the business model they followed began with experiments in the voluntary sector. British holiday camps owe their history to a range of operators with philanthropic and collective as well as commercial aims.

Round bell tents were the forerunners of chalets, first transferred from a military setting in the late nineteenth century to provide poor city children with a taste of outdoor life. Such charitable endeavours may seem a world away from Redcoats and Glamorous Granny competitions but they were the first to demonstrate the potential of cheap seaside holidays in a camp setting. Joseph and Elizabeth Cunningham, pioneers of the self-contained holiday resort, began by organising summer camps for underprivileged boys from Liverpool. They consistently failed to cover their costs, so in 1894 Joseph was relieved of his post as Superintendent of the Florence Institute in Toxteth. The Presbyterian couple continued to run their camp on the Isle of Man, but operating as a business required them to make a profit. To give paying campers a real holiday, they replaced drills and tent inspections with an open-air hotel service.

Until its closure in 1945 Cunningham's Camp was open to men only, all of whom had to sign a pledge not to touch alcohol or use improper language. Despite these strictures, the camp quickly outgrew its rented site. The season ran from May to October and at peak times each bell tent accommodated eight men, their beds arranged like spokes of a wheel around the central pole.

Opposite: Snapshots of Edwardian campers posing outside their holiday accommodation at the all-male Cunningham's Holiday Camp. The bell tents were cared for and repaired by the camp's sailmaker, who had his own workshop.

The huge dining pavilion at Cunningham's Isle of Man camp had a roof terrace punctuated by little turrets in the best tradition of seaside exoticism, and a glazed lower level complete with mock-Tudor gables.

More tents could be pitched to meet increasing demand but the camp's capacity was limited to six hundred by the size of the marquees used as dining and recreation rooms. With profits to reinvest, the Cunninghams looked around for their own plot and in 1904 moved their 'Canvas City' on to 5 acres at Little Switzerland, nearer the Isle of Man's main town of Douglas.

The new camp's centrepiece was a 100-foot-long dining pavilion with room to feed 1,600 men at one sitting. Commercial success allowed an ever-expanding range of on-site facilities, including darkrooms, miniature golf, a swimming pool heated by exhaust steam from the camp's own generators, a concert hall and a cinema. Even the washroom block had pretensions, its utilitarian function disguised by the battlements of a miniature castle. Establishing a golden rule for future holiday camps, the Cunninghams kept the sleeping accommodation simple so as to maintain an affordable all-inclusive tariff.

The *Camp Herald* was produced every year for distribution to prospective campers with pictures, testimonials and reassuring advice for those who had never been away from home. By 1938 Cunningham's could accommodate four thousand men at a time.

In addition, tent life helped create a sense of companionship that transcended different social backgrounds. Middle- and working-class men joined in singing the camp song, and to the refrain 'Are we downhearted?' the response would loudly come back in the negative. 'Are we coming back again? Yes!'

Fostering a sense of community was crucial to the emergent holiday camp ethos and John Fletcher Dodd was among the first to realise its potency. He began in 1906 with three bell tents and ten trade unionist friends who came from London's East End to the Norfolk coast. In the same year Dodd formed a Great Yarmouth branch of the Independent Labour Party and, reasoning that working-class men on holiday by the sea would provide a captive audience for the discussion of his socialist ideals, he bought more tents. For reasons of philosophy and economy, the campers staffed the site themselves; an early advertisement stressed that 'It is an example of collective effort where all help and all share'. The Socialist Holiday Camp combined campfire singsongs and story-telling with debates and talks. Highlight of the week was the Sunday evening lecture, guest speakers including George Bernard Shaw, Keir Hardie and Bertrand Russell.

A firm teetotaller like Cunningham, Dodd banned liquor, swearing and gambling. He also ruled that there was to be no talking in tents after 11 p.m., and campers who were late to meals were liable for a fine. Such regulations were laid down to ensure the camp's smooth running and they did nothing to hinder its growth. Ultimately, the high demand for places led to upgraded accommodation and a paid workforce to cater for a clientele increasingly drawn from the professional and business classes. By 1912 Dodd had purchased more land and filled it with rows of 8-foot-square wooden huts, each with its own cold-water tap. As idealism gave way to commercial realism, the 'Socialist' title was replaced by the place-specific name of 'Caister Holiday Camp'. When John Fletcher Dodd died aged ninety in 1952 more than a thousand holidaymakers a week were staying at his site.

Camps with a social conscience proved to be more viable when run by co-operative societies and trade unions, bodies in which potential campers already had a stake. In 1911 the Renfrewshire and United Co-operative Baking Society leased a farm at Roseland, overlooking Rothesay Bay, and erected bell tents to

> Don't forget the Socialist Camp, Caister-on-Sea, opens May 1st.
>
> Is run by Socialists to help forward Socialism.
>
> It is an example of collective effort where all help and all share.
>
> Provides a healthful and invigorating holiday at a nominal price.
>
> The whole of the surplus profit is devoted to the cause.
>
> *Apply Hon. Sec.*, J. FLETCHER DODD.

John Fletcher Dodd's aims are clearly stated in this advertisement for his Norfolk holiday camp, c. 1910.

Early camps began to issue badges so that campers could identify each other easily and staff could ensure that only paid-up club members enjoyed the free amenities. The Caister badge shows the founder, J. Fletcher Dodd, smoking his pipe. It cost 2d.

CAMP SHOP, CAISTER CAMP

In the 1930s the Caister camp shop sold bathing costumes, hired out tennis rackets and provided a twenty-four hour developing and printing service for photographs. It also served as a useful meeting point.

test the enthusiasm of members. An overwhelmingly positive response led them to purchase and improve the site. After the First World War chalets were built for four hundred guests, and the camp did not finally close until 1974. On the North Wales coast near Rhyl, the Coventry Co-operative Society ran its own holiday camp from 1930. The first co-operators to arrive at Voryd, on Kinmel Bay, found a motley ensemble of accommodation: six huts, an old railway carriage, an ex-army hut, twenty-four square tents and a few old bell tents. It did not matter; with everyone wanting to get away at the same time, places had to be balloted for and people queued in the February chill just to put their names down at the Co-op offices.

These regional experiments were in the vanguard and by the time the Co-operative Wholesale Society and the Workers' Travel Association joined forces as Travco in 1938 holiday camps were very much in vogue. Travco planned to build six camps for families who lacked the means to visit commercial sites, but the only one completed was Rogerson Hall at Corton, 3 miles north of Lowestoft, opening in August that year. Its Modern-style buildings could accommodate three hundred adults, and each person who stayed for a week or more was entitled to nominate a deserving case for a free holiday. Though well-intentioned, the camp was rapidly booked up by school teachers and minor civil servants.

White-collar workers were quick to assume the holiday camp habit. W. J. Brown relished the freedom of staying in a bell tent at Caister Holiday

THE DANCE HALL

ROGERSON HALL HOLIDAY CAMP

ROGERSON HALL FROM SOUTH.

THE CHALETS.

Behind the modern reception block of Travco's Rogerson Hall two wings splayed out in a 'V' shape housing the social room and dance hall. To the rear were back-to-back chalets in flat-roofed dormitory blocks.

An aerial photograph, taken in 1937, of the first Civil Service Holiday Camp, situated just above the beach at Corton, near Lowestoft. This view shows how the chalets were built around the recreation grounds and tennis courts.

Camp during his youth and later used his influence as general secretary of the Civil Service Clerical Association to promote the idea to members. After his executive committee pulled out, Brown raised the funds to build Corton Civil Service Camp himself. His risk paid off. Accommodation, priced at two guineas per adult per week, was fully booked for the 1924 season and, when he was forced to turn would-be campers away the

Croyde Bay
Holiday Camp in
North Devon,
pictured soon
after its acquisition
by the National
Association of
Local Government
Officers in 1931.

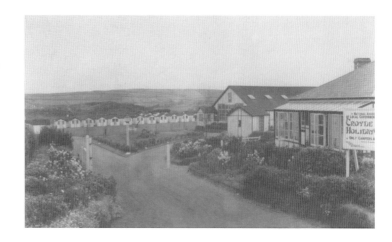

In 1938 the
original wooden
chalets at Croyde
Bay were upgraded
to brick bungalows
with hot and cold
running water.
A new concert hall
with a stage and
dance floor was
added at the same
time.

following year, Brown looked for another site. The second Civil Service
camp opened on Hayling Island in 1930. In that same year the National
Association of Local Government Officers (NALGO) agreed to build a
holiday camp for its members. A committee was appointed and the perfect
site was found – a newly built commercial camp at Croyde Bay in North
Devon. The existing management team stayed on and from April 1931
NALGO members were making use of the ninety-five asbestos huts,
dining-hall, recreation room, tennis court and putting green. In 1933 a

second camp opened at Cayton Bay near Scarborough, this time built to the union's own specifications.

The most ambitious occupational camp in the country opened at Skegness in May 1939. Built at a cost of £35,000, it was available to the mineworkers of Derbyshire – some forty thousand men and their families – thanks to a welfare fund supported through a levy on every ton of coal they raised. Reduced fares negotiated with railway and bus companies meant that the nine hundred visitors arriving every Saturday paid just 24s 6d each for their entire week's holiday. To make the most of this facility, Derbyshire pit-owners agreed to adopt the 'spread-over system', staggering their holiday shutdowns. Construction work was still in progress when Sir Frederick Sykes, Chairman of the Miners' Welfare Fund, performed the opening ceremony, officially unlocking one of the finished chalets. In his speech Sir Frederick stressed the importance of the project and, having earlier paid a visit to Butlin's 'luxury holiday camp' just along the Lincolnshire coast, expressed his hope that 'the Derbyshire camp, when completed, would be as well done, if not better'.

When planning his camps, Billy Butlin had travelled to the Isle of Man to see how Cunningham's catered for the large numbers he hoped to attract himself. By the 1930s commercial and non-commercial holiday camps were operating literally side by side, borrowing from and competing with each other in a way that ensured the concept evolved.

A 1950s brochure for NALGO's two holiday centres. The Yorkshire camp ultimately proved unviable and was sold in 1976. The Devon site remains open under the auspices of NALGO's successor, Unison.

GOING MASS MARKET

THE OPTIMISTIC MOOD of the inter-war years found visual representation in Art Deco, Hollywood movies and Modernism. Fashion and health were combined in new open-air pursuits like sunbathing at the lido or hiking to a youth hostel. The holiday camp brought these things together and packaged them for a mass market. So quickly did the concept spread that in 1935 the National Federation of Permanent Holiday Camps was launched to establish industry standards. Their membership criteria codified what the term 'holiday camp' had come to mean: full-board accommodation in permanent huts; on-site water supply and sanitary system; plus dining and dance halls large enough to cater for all campers.

By summer 1938 Britain had around 150 holiday camps, mostly set up during the preceding few years, and able to accommodate an estimated forty thousand people at one time. Critics feared the coastline was being disfigured by the unrelenting spread of chalets, and there were certainly notable concentrations: there were fourteen holiday camps along a 10-mile stretch of coastline either side of the Norfolk–Suffolk border. During the last two years of the decade a dedicated publication, the *Holiday Camp Review*, charted the rapid progress of this leisure development, and proof that it had arrived as a new building type came in 1939 with an exhibition of holiday camp designs and extensive features in the architectural press.

Many inter-war holiday camps were small, family-run concerns, often built in the grounds of mansions, the house itself becoming part of the amenities. Others were built from scratch on a massive scale. Customer loyalty was high and such men as Fletcher Dodd, Herbert 'Pa' Potter, 'Maddy' Maddieson, Captain Warner and Billy Butlin set themselves up as paternalistic proprietors, the sort of men you could have a drink with and whose friendly holiday camp family you wanted to remain a part of. Both Potter, a staunch socialist inspired by Fletcher Dodd's endeavour, and Maddieson went into business on the Norfolk coast. After being demobbed from the army, Potter used prize money won in newspaper competitions to launch his own holiday camp at Hemsby. He opened in 1920 with timber huts instead of tents but

Opposite:
A 1939 brochure for Prestatyn declared that 'As the word "camp" cannot convey one fraction of the amenities, we have christened it "The Chalet Village by the Sea".' At night the Art Deco lettering over the entrance gates lit up in red and blue neon.

Energetic young campers and a sunburst motif are used to present Corton Beach Holiday Camp as a fashionably healthy destination in 1939. The brochure promised 'glorious golden sands ... lapped by sun-drenched blue waters' just north of Lowestoft.

sold up just four years later to begin anew south of Great Yarmouth at Hopton. Still unsatisfied, Potter launched the new Hopton Beach Camp in 1933, the chalets and main buildings, including a 'lavishly furnished' sun-lounge, now built of brick. He promoted it as 'The luxury camp with moderate charges and a fine camp spirit'. It was to be that mixture of luxury, affordability and camaraderie that carried holiday camps through the next three decades.

Permanent chalets built of brick were a selling point of 'Pa' Potter's Hopton Beach camp from 1933.

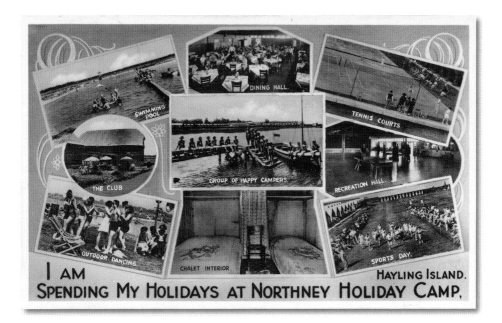

I AM
SPENDING MY HOLIDAYS AT NORTHNEY HOLIDAY CAMP, HAYLING ISLAND.

When Captain Harry Warner opened his first holiday camp in 1931 his aim was to provide a week's holiday for less than a week's wage. He had moved to Hayling Island, Hampshire, in 1925 after taking early retirement from the Royal Artillery and there set up a business selling ice-cream to day trippers. Witnessing the success of W. J. Brown's second Civil Service holiday camp, Warner purchased Northney Farm and set about converting it for up-market camping. The main barn became a restaurant, where four-course meals were served by tail-coated waiters; the outbuildings served as a bar and entertainments room. One hundred wooden chalets were built and an area of the sea was fenced off to create a swimming pool. In 1932 Butlin-Warner Holiday Services was formed to develop a new camp at Seaton in Devon, the pair having met as a result of Billy Butlin's amusement park on Hayling Island. It proved a short-lived partnership but Warner continued to expand his business, building new camps at Dovercourt in Essex in 1936 and at Puckpool Park on the Isle of Wight in 1938.

Butlin meanwhile was pursuing his dream of huge holiday camps for middle-income families, with high-quality communal spaces and entertainment. He was a consummate showman and shrewd businessman, already wealthy after a decade building up his coastal amusements empire. Born in Cape Town in 1899, Butlin had a peripatetic youth, moving around the world and gaining little formal education. After moving to Canada with his mother, the young Billy worked as a commercial artist for Eaton's

Views of Captain Harry Warner's first camp at Northney Farm, Hayling Island. This postcard was sent in July 1938 by Dorrie; she was enjoying her stay despite the dull weather and was pleased to report that Peggy 'has first prize for best ankles'.

15

Toronto department store and attended the company's summer camp. He served with the Canadian Army during the First World War, but a strong sense of his West Country roots drew him back to England and his mother's fairground family. His uncle set him up with a hoop-la stand and from the start Butlin pushed for bigger profits. When trade moved away from traditional fairs to the seaside, Butlin moved with it, setting up his stall at Skegness in 1927. Negotiating the United Kingdom rights for dodgem cars in the following year allowed him to conquer other resorts and secure the amusement concessions at London's Olympia. By 1933 he had nine hundred men in his permanent employment and two thousand during the six-month summer season. It was this labour force that would build his first holiday camp, outside Skegness.

In August 1935 the *Skegness Evening News* raved about Billy Butlin's 'ultra-modern development'. The six hundred projected chalets would form a 'wonderful miniature garden suburb' with 'Free boating, free bathing, free golf, free tennis, free bowls, free orchestral music and free instruction in physical culture for 1,000 guests every week!' His luxury holiday camp was far from complete when Butlin ran a half-page advertisement in the *Daily Express* but so many enquiries and deposits flooded in that the season was almost fully booked from the start. All the planning, the design of the buildings and their interiors was down to Butlin himself. At the centre of the site was the entrance pavilion, a large steel-framed structure clad in brick and crisply rendered in white stucco. The style was avowedly Modern, if lacking the purity required for approval by the architectural press. To either side, more large buildings housed dining-rooms, bars and dance-halls. This was the age of neon, a transfer of bright lights from the fairground to mass entertainment venues, and the 1936 brochure assured potential campers that 'no-one is more conscious of this than Mr Butlin'. Lit up in red along the reception block was a phrase from Shakespeare's *A Midsummer Night's Dream*: 'Our true intent is all for your delight.'

This architect's impression demonstrates the scale of Billy Butlin's ambition for his first camp, built from 1936 facing the main coast road north of Skegness. Chalet lines stretch towards the sea behind a row of huge communal buildings.

A London visitor, among the first to visit Butlin's for Easter 1936, was asked by the *Skegness Evening News* if he had tried other camps: 'Oh, yes, several on the South Coast, but they are crude stone-age affairs compared with this one. I guess Mr Butlin will soon have to think of extending.' By the outbreak of war the Lincolnshire site had capacity for 4,500 and would ultimately have enough accommodation for double that figure. A second Butlin's camp opened at Clacton, Essex, in 1938 and a third east coast venture at Filey in Yorkshire was projected for the 1940 season. Demand was proved but there was more to it, as the *Daily News Chronicle* observed in June 1937:

> Thousands of people are having a New Kind of Holiday ... A major social phenomenon is making its appearance all over the face of Britain, altering the age-old manner of the English holiday ... The name of the phenomenon is – 'The Holiday Camp'.

The father of them all, Cunningham's, was also moving with the times and by 1936 was averaging 60,000 campers a year. Its focus on outdoor activities and camaraderie was in tune with the times but the men who arrived in the

The cocktail bar at Skegness was described by the *Observer* as 'streamlined, chromium plated, Odeon cinema *modernismus* (a pet decor of Butlin's)'. Nesting chairs made of tubular steel completed the look of mass-market luxury.

1920s and 1930s were notably more sophisticated than their predecessors. Even before the First World War, campers were served their meals by smartly dressed waiters as the camp orchestra played in the background. Now came innovations, such as the electric escalator that carried campers up the hill from Douglas and, after Joseph Cunningham's death, morning and evening dances to which women were allowed. Alcohol was still banned but an alternative was offered by the latest novelty from Prohibition Era America, the soda fountain.

As Hollywood movies reached mass audiences in Art Deco cinemas, American style became synonymous with the future. In 1938 tour company Thomas Cook Ltd joined forces with the London Midland & Scottish Railway (LMS) to establish a chain of up-to-date holiday camps inspired by Modern movement design in Britain and the United States. The only one built was at Prestatyn in North Wales, designed by LMS architect William Hamlyn. At the opening ceremony Lord Stamp dubbed it the 'Everyman's Luxury Hotel' though in reality it was aimed at Thomas Cook's existing middle-class clientele; the weekly price was similar to the

Railway posters embody the inter-war leisure aesthetic. The London & North Eastern Railway paid half of Butlin's advertising costs, so it was no coincidence that his second camp at Clacton was also on their line.

BUTLIN'S HOLIDAY CAMP
CLACTON-ON-SEA
IT'S QUICKER BY RAIL
ILLUSTRATED BOOKLET FREE FROM R. P. BUTLIN'S PUBLICITY DEPARTMENT, SKEGNESS, OR ANY L·N·E·R OFFICE OR AGENCY

3½ guineas charged by Butlin at Skegness. An aesthetic and commercial success, Prestatyn gained a level of coverage in the architectural press that was unique among holiday camps. The open-air heart of the camp was the Sun Court, where a kiosk surrounded by coloured parasols and fountains was overlooked by a 60-foot-high observation tower. To one side was the reception block; to the other a massive structure comprising a dining-room with space for all 1,750 guests, and a ballroom for six hundred couples. The swimming pool lay between the Sun Court and the Prestatyn Clipper, a ship-shaped

Left: From 1923 an electric elevator carried Cunningham's campers up the steep incline from Douglas Promenade. Tickets were bought from the camp post office 'by the yard'.

Below: Modernist architecture on the Flintshire coast. A view across Prestatyn's Sun Court towards the reception block and observation tower. It cost 3d to climb to the top.

... and so cheap too!

What a wonderful camp Prestatyn is! So bright, so spacious, and as clean as a new pin. And what a beautiful situation, too, right on the sea front, by a stretch of lovely golden sands and an extensive newly-built promenade. Not that you'll always want to sit by the seashore, there's so much on in the camp, fun at the splendid swimming pool, deck games on the famous "Clipper" by the children's paddling pool, sports of all kinds, tennis, bowls, cricket, and netball on the spacious playing fields, dancing, a continuous round of entertainments, and a delightful children's corner, where kiddies can be left in safety while parents enjoy themselves. There is no camp in Britain which has such lovely pavilions or such well-built and well-fitted chalets. They are superb, lit up by a blaze of flower-beds, and trim green lawns. Sitting under a gay umbrella in the Sun Court by the lily pool, you might be in the South of France.

FROM £8·10·0 A WEEK ALL IN

and special rates for children

The ship-shaped Prestatyn Clipper made a perfect backdrop to the camp's open-air pool. Its bar featured lamps from an ocean liner and bollards from Newfoundland schooners. Outside, there was rigging and a teak deck for playing quoits.

bar that capitalised on the fashionable ocean-liner aesthetic. With its connotations of luxurious modernity, the Clipper featured strongly in camp publicity, prompting the 1952 brochure slogan, 'All aboard for a real seaside holiday!'

Further up the west coast, near Morecambe, Middleton Tower Luxury Holiday Camp adopted the catchphrase 'Cruising on land' to promote its liner-themed buildings. Harry S. Kamiya had plans to rival Billy Butlin and already did so in amusements, running Luna Park in his home town of Blackpool and twenty-five other concessions around the country. He proposed to create a holiday camp for three thousand people on an 80-acre site. The project was due to be completed in 1940 but owing to the outbreak of war it never reached its full capacity. The first phase, however, opened in August 1939 with eight hundred chalets for a thousand campers. As the

The real *Berengaria* liner was scrapped in 1938, having been run by Cunard since arriving from Germany as reparation for the wartime loss of the *Lusitania*. Its fittings were reused at Middleton Tower for a fashionable 'cruising on land' effect.

Morecambe and Heysham Visitor reported, the main buildings had been 'constructed to represent the decks of liners, with masts and funnels on the roof ... To add to the nautical effect, panelling and furnishings from the luxury liners *Berengaria* and *Leviathan* have been used for the sun lounge, palm court, ballroom and banquet hall.' At one time the largest passenger vessel in the world, the *Berengaria*'s fixtures and fittings gave a true transatlantic glamour to Middleton Tower.

Squires Gate camp brought a taste of California to Blackpool. All the buildings were rendered in rough cream plaster with red tile roofs and bright blue woodwork.

Corner of Ballroom, Squire's Gate Holiday Beach.

The lavish ballroom at Squires Gate was probably designed by Andrew Mazzei, Art Director of the Gaumont Film Company. He also worked at Blackpool Winter Gardens and lived locally.

Just south of Blackpool, Squires Gate Holiday Camp took its architectural inspiration direct from Hollywood, as its owner, Herbert Pye, had lived on America's Pacific coast. Begun as a simple camping ground, Squires Gate had by 1933 a camp store, a café and a fish and chip shop to cater for the five thousand people it could accommodate under canvas. More significant improvements were to come as Pye set out to create a fully fledged holiday camp. Lancashire sweetheart Gracie Fields opened the new camp chapel in 1937; touring the site, complete with its 1,400 chalets, she declared: 'You aren't half going to be posh here.' Two years later, a huge new dining-hall, grand piazza and club bar were added, all in the Spanish mission style beloved of Californian architects. Guests could imagine themselves transported thousands of miles away to a holiday in movie-land; Pye even employed the art director of a film studio to decorate some of the interiors.

On 3 September 1939 holidaymakers were pulled sharply back to reality by the declaration of war. Men had been receiving their call-up papers throughout the summer and Tannoy announcements at Butlin's had suffered constant interruptions as the names of guests who had to return home were broadcast. With their high-volume accommodation units and open spaces, holiday camps around the country were immediately requisitioned for military use. Within days, Butlin's Skegness had become the naval training ship HMS *Royal Arthur*, its brightly coloured chalets painted battleship grey. In a shrewd bargain with the government, Billy

BUTLIN'S HOLIDAY CAMP, FILEY

THE SWIMMING POO[L]

Butlin completed his half-finished camp at Filey and built two new military camps on a favourable post-war buy-back arrangement. His first Welsh camp at Pwllheli came into being as a result, as did that at Ayr facing the Isle of Arran. Meanwhile Fred Pontin, who had yet to enter the holiday camp business, was getting his first taste of mass catering through a Ministry of Supply posting in the Orkneys, supervising the meals for workers building oil containers and dummy ships. He subsequently took

Selling mass-market glamour in the 1940s. The open-air pool at Butlin's Filey fills the picture, and figures in the foreground look like movie pin-ups.

BUTLIN'S FILEY
Sight-seeing on a Camp Train

Filey Holiday Camp station opened in May 1947. Campers and their luggage were transferred from railway to reception by the land train pictured here. Butlin's camps were so big that these trains also took sightseeing tours.

23

PONTIN CAMPS

"SMALL UNIT"
Carefree Holidays

SUSSEX · BRACKLESHAM BAY · CHICHESTER
SOMERSET · WESTON-SUPER-MARE
BREAN SANDS AND SAND BAY
DORSET · OSMINGTON BAY · WEYMOUTH
SOUTH DEVON · PAIGNTON · TORQUAY
NORTH DEVON · BUCKLEIGH · WESTWARD HO!

Write for Combined Brochure to :—

PONTIN'S HOLIDAY CAMPS KING'S ASH HILL · PAIGNTON · DEVON
TELEPHONE PAIGNTON 59984-5 MEMBERS OF THE NATIONAL FEDERATION OF PERMANENT HOLIDAY CAMPS

A flyer from 1955 advertises the six holiday camps Fred Pontin had acquired since the end of the Second World War. While stressing his camps as 'small unit' sites, Pontin is also showing all the expected facilities and entertainments.

over a troublesome National Service hostel near Kidderminster, where male forge workers and land girls lived in chalets. By improving living conditions, food and entertainment, Pontin learnt valuable lessons about how to keep lots of people happy at once.

Pontin realised that the pent-up desire for holidays would be huge when peace returned. In 1939 government research indicated that 11 million workers were entitled to the newly introduced statutory week of paid holiday. After the war there was full employment. Families would be looking for an affordable break near the beaches that had been out of bounds for five years. In spring 1946 Pontin bought Brean Sands, an established holiday camp near Burnham-on-Sea in Somerset, and, by pitching his weekly price at less than the average working man's wage, it was soon full. Within weeks he had purchased its sister camp at Osmington Bay near Weymouth. The following year he acquired four more sites: Sand Bay at Weston-super-Mare, Buckleigh Place at Westward Ho!, the South Devon Holiday Camp near Paignton and Bracklesham Bay in Sussex. Pontin was now marketing 1,300 accommodation units over six locations, compared to Butlin's five camps offering more than 30,000 bed spaces. The two entrepreneurs worked in friendly rivalry; Pontin's camps were always cheaper, its smaller sites benefiting from lower overheads, while the huge size of Butlin's sites gave campers more choice of entertainments. Harry Warner was also expanding his empire, taking over the Civil Service camps at Corton and Southleigh, Hayling Island, as well as building a new modern centre in concrete, glass and steel at St Clare on the Isle of Wight.

By the 1950s holiday camps had become symbolic of post-war society, offering leisure for all at a high standard and a reasonable price. It was boom time and in the 1960s the big operators got even bigger. To complete his national coverage, Butlin built three new camps: at Bognor Regis, Sussex, in 1960; at Minehead, Somerset, two years later; and at Barry Island, South Wales, in 1966. Warners went from eight camps in 1960 to eleven by 1965; Pontin's continued its acquisition and make-over policy, adding Prestatyn, Middleton Tower and Squires Gate to a portfolio that comprised sixteen camps by the end of the decade.

A young London family ride around Warner's Corton camp together in 1947. These 'sociable cycles' were a perfect expression of the communal holiday camp ethos.

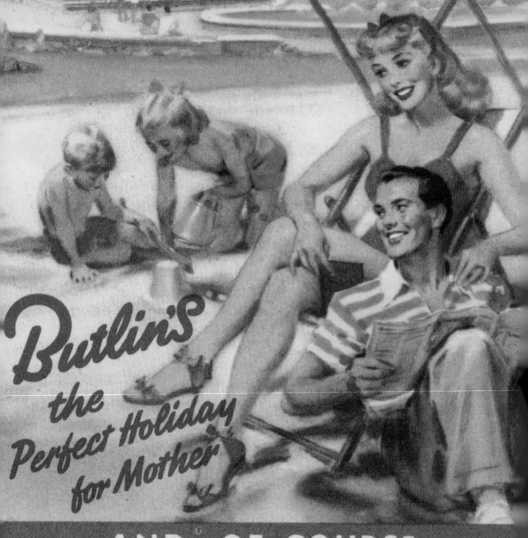

Butlin's the Perfect Holiday for Mother

AND, OF COURSE, THE REST OF THE FAMILY, TOO

FREE BOOKLET

As well as sharing her children's pleasur
at Butlin's, mother may from time t
time leave them happy in safe hands an
have the chance to feel a bride again
recapturing with her husband the magi
of their earlier years together amid a
the delights and attractions of thei
Butlin holiday.

BUTLIN'S LTD., DEPT. H.B. 439 OXFORD STREET, LONDON, W

THE ALL-IN PACKAGE

BILLY BUTLIN cited his experience of a wet week in a Barry Island boarding house as one of the reasons he went into the holiday camp business. The traditional seaside landlady did not always conform to the stereotype of a battleaxe in carpet slippers but her brand of holiday accommodation was increasingly out of step with the leisure aspirations of working people. Having treated himself to a rare break in the early 1920s, Butlin was astonished at how unwelcome he and his fellow guests were made to feel. 'We had to leave the premises after breakfast and were not encouraged to return until lunch-time.' It had yet to become standard practice for guests to have their own keys, so everyone had to submit to this routine, leaving again after lunch and returning in the evening for dinner. This was all very well in fine weather but in the rain it was miserable. 'And it rained incessantly all the time I was on Barry Island. I felt sorry for myself,' remembered Butlin, 'but I felt even sorrier for the families with young children as they trudged around wet and bedraggled, or forlornly filled in time in amusement arcades until they could return to their boarding houses.' When holiday camps advertised themselves as free and easy, go-as-you-please destinations, they were doing so as an alternative to the established seaside model.

Despite the huge capacity of commercial holiday camps, accommodation in separate chalets led pre-war commentators to recognise an inherent regard for privacy in this new phenomenon. When campers arrived with their luggage at the reception building, they handed over the balance of their payment and were given the all-important chalet key. The luxury of personal, lockable space could not be overestimated. It allowed people to be sociable when they wanted to and to opt out when they did not. So many activities were provided on site that chalets were primarily designed for sleeping, and different combinations of double beds, single beds and cots were available, the booking form for Prestatyn running to nine options. In each case the price was the same and there was no single supplement. Chalet maids were employed to make the beds and tidy up so that campers did not have to. Wash basins were provided at a time when this was extremely unusual in boarding

Opposite:
An example
of how 1950s
holiday camp
advertising
appealed directly
to women.
Mothers were
offered the chance
to 'feel a bride
again', thanks to
free childcare.

houses and, though most only had cold water, there were communal taps available for hot. Toilets and baths were located in blocks at the end of chalet lines, labelled 'Lads' and 'Lasses' by Butlin as if to stress the informality of the new holiday environment. Guests wondering what to pack were asked to bring only their own towels and soap. Clothes could be stored in wardrobes and chests of drawers or behind fabric screens that matched the curtains. Complete with electric lighting, the chalet experience was quite different to tent camping though early guests presumably suffered some misapprehensions on this score as the 1939 brochure for Butlin's Skegness found it necessary to specify that stoves and spirit lamps were not allowed.

Prestatyn chalets were of a modern design in keeping with the camp's communal buildings. They were built to form courtyards with bathroom blocks in the centre.

Most early chalets tended to be detached, the long blocks of double-decker examples coming in from the late 1950s and 1960s. Even Cunningham's upgraded from bell tents in 1936, introducing 'chalet tents' with their own front doors and more headroom. Squires Gate also had a sort of halfway house, offering cheaper wooden chalets with roofs made of stretched canvas alongside more permanent Californian-style huts. Pitching his product at middle-income campers, Billy Butlin adopted the mock

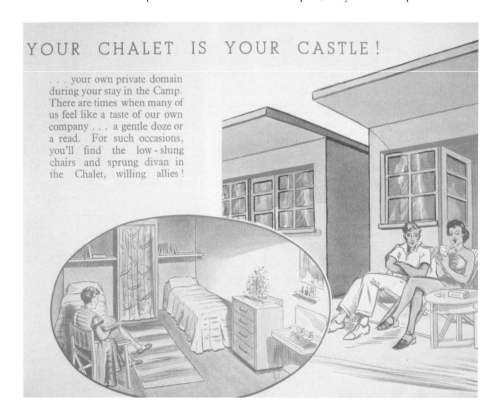

YOUR CHALET IS YOUR CASTLE!

. . . your own private domain during your stay in the Camp. There are times when many of us feel like a taste of our own company . . . a gentle doze or a read. For such occasions, you'll find the low-slung chairs and sprung divan in the Chalet, willing allies!

Blackpool had a tradition of cheap apartment accommodation where guests provided their own food, so Squires Gate Holiday Camp offered a low-cost chalet with kitchen and 'dining section'. The camp beds had straw mattresses.

timber-framing of inter-war suburbia with his so-called 'Elizabethan' chalets. Each one cost £10 to build and measured 10 feet square. The construction method was directed at mass production; timber frames were covered in a mesh of chicken wire lined on the inside with plywood and rendered with cement on the outside. Since plants and flowers formed a key element in Billy Butlin's vision of an attractive camp, every chalet was to have its own little garden. Unfortunately, real rose bowers took time to grow, so during the first season workmen had to paint them on to the chalet walls. Bright colours were another fundamental of Butlin's design philosophy, particularly crucial in creating a cheerful holiday atmosphere after the war. At the opening

A family is shown to the bright pink and blue Tudor-style chalet they will call home for a week. Publicity image from Butlin's Pwllheli brochure of 1958.

29

of Pwllheli camp in 1947, a reporter for the *Guardian* described 'indigo blue chalets with light blue doors and orange curtains. There are fawn chalets with green doors. In fact there are chalets and shops and cafés and cinemas and theatres and ballrooms of every conceivable colour.'

When Fred and Bertha Wood decided to turn their Ivy House campsite at Blackpool into a holiday camp they booked a week at Butlin's Skegness and spent their time watching the workmen putting up chalets. The method was not hard to reproduce with a concrete mixer, spades and trowels, and they rapidly erected four blocks of four chalets with white walls and red roofs. Bertha made frilled counterpanes and matching floral curtains to brighten the interiors. A different approach was followed on the Isle of Wight, where an Irishman named O'Hea imported cedarwood from Canada to build

Illustrations from 1938 of 'The famous Sunnyvale Holiday Chalets' at Kinmel Bay near Rhyl. A choice of six different types included multi-room chalets and double chalets with private shower, bath and WC. Every chalet had its own verandah.

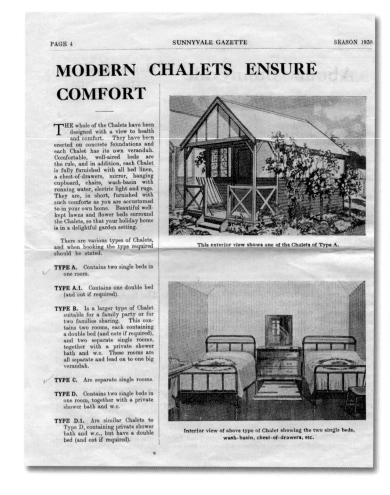

PAGE 4   SUNNYVALE GAZETTE   SEASON 1938

MODERN CHALETS ENSURE COMFORT

THE whole of the Chalets have been designed with a view to health and comfort. They have been erected on concrete foundations and each Chalet has its own verandah. Comfortable, well-aired beds are the rule, and in addition, each Chalet is fully furnished with all bed linen, a chest-of-drawers, mirror, hanging cupboard, chairs, wash-basin with running water, electric light and rugs. They are, in short, furnished with such comforts as you are accustomed to in your own home. Beautiful well-kept lawns and flower beds surround the Chalets, so that your holiday home is in a delightful garden setting.

There are various types of Chalets, and when booking the type required should be stated.

TYPE A. Contains two single beds in one room.

TYPE A.1. Contains one double bed (and cot if required).

TYPE B. Is a larger type of Chalet suitable for a family party or for two families sharing. This contains two rooms, each containing a double bed (and cots if required), and two separate single rooms, together with a private shower bath and w.c. These rooms are all separate and lead on to one big verandah.

TYPE C. Are separate single rooms.

TYPE D. Contains two single beds in one room, together with a private shower bath and w.c.

TYPE D.1. Are similar Chalets to Type D, containing private shower bath and w.c., but have a double bed (and cot if required).

This exterior view shows one of the Chalets of Type A.

Interior view of above type of Chalet showing the two single beds, wash-basin, chest-of-drawers, etc.

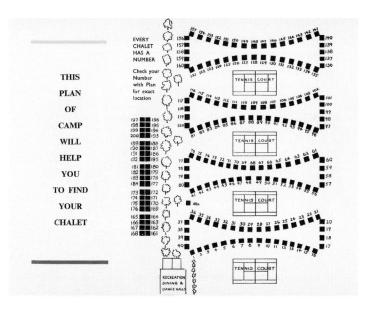

The unusual chalet layout at Golden Sands, Hopton, near Great Yarmouth. In 1955 accommodation was available for 460 people – 'enough to make a merry time, yet there's always plenty of room'.

log cabins on a 36-acre site of woodland between Ryde and Cowes. Propped up on stilts, these huts were admired by *The Builder* for their 'hefty and rough' qualities, a world away from Butlin's polite suburban style. Owing to force of circumstance, the first Pontin's chalets were also rather rough and ready, the existing wooden huts at Brean Sands being fitted out to a basic standard with war surplus from the Ministry of Supply. To young couples who had married during the uncertain conditions of wartime this did not matter; they gratefully closed the chalet door and enjoyed their first taste of domestic privacy.

Days at Caister Holiday Camp began when the tea urn was wheeled around the chalets at 7 o'clock. Half an hour later the dressing bell rang and breakfast was served at 8 a.m. Cooking for large numbers required a high degree of organisation, so the morning routine was a pragmatic way of ensuring that campers were all ready for their bacon and eggs at the same time. Butlin's camps were so large that every

Early morning tea service at Prestatyn in the late 1950s. Campers bought books of tear-off tickets from the Britannia Bar and handed them to maids dressed in green and yellow uniforms, which matched the chalet paintwork.

31

meal was served in two sittings, making it doubly important that people were at the dining hall for their allocated breakfast slot. In characteristic fashion Billy Butlin used camp spirit to disguise this administrative necessity, making his alarm call into a jolly song:

Roll out of bed in the morning
With a big, big smile and a good, good morning.
You'll find life is worth while
If you roll out of bed with a smile.

The sound of Radio Butlin crackling into life via the Tannoy speakers cemented into chalet walls could doubtless become annoying, particularly for those who were on the second sitting for breakfast, and the frequency with which maintenance men were called to repair cut speaker wires attests to this. Many thousands of campers simply put up with it as part of the package and probably took the view that as they had paid for breakfast they might as well make sure they ate it. Butlin's formula for effective camper management did not suit everyone and from the early days camps had to defend themselves against snobbery and contemptuous criticisms of over-organisation. The implication was always that rules took away a person's holiday freedom when for many campers the reverse was true. Not having to think about what and when to eat provided a genuine break from the workaday routine.

Radio Butlin made its last morning call in 1979. Because of the knock-on effect on meal schedules, there was hell to pay if security staff failed to wake the Redcoat announcer in good time.

In the 1930s 'full board' meant four meals: breakfast, dinner, tea and supper. After the war this was reduced to three, with cafés and snack bars on site to fill hunger gaps for an additional fee. In the large dining-rooms campers were served by teams of waiters and waitresses, quickly striking up a friendly repartee with the servers they saw at every mealtime. Most camps could feed everyone on site in one go but waitresses at Butlin's worked an exhausting ten and a half-hour day, serving six times with only a half-hour between the two sittings in which to clear away, wash up and re-lay the tables. The first historian of English holiday habits, J. A. R. Pimlott, visited Butlin's Clacton in August 1946 and noted that 'Lunch was an impressive demonstration of efficiency. I ate at the Kent House second sitting – in a huge well-lit restaurant ... The service was speedy, and the food was good. Soup – meat pie and vegetables – steamed pudding – it was a mass-produced meal but substantial and well enough prepared. No bread – owing to rationing.' Though coupons were still being clipped from ration books until 1954, holiday camps did their best to provide a week off from post-war shortages.

When it came to mass catering, Cunningham's Isle of Man camp was a pioneer once again, able to feed up to 3,600 diners in one sitting with food grown and prepared on site. Vegetables came from the camp farm, as did milk, supplied by more than a hundred camp cows. The bakehouse and butcher's shop were manned around the clock. Kitchen gadgetry included

At Ayr, campers were woken by pipers for the full Scottish experience. Bagpipes announced every mealtime and Redcoats wore kilts. The double-decker chalets Butlin introduced to camps in the 1960s, however, had more of a cuckoo clock aesthetic.

A specimen menu from Cunningham's Holiday Camp, c. 1937. Dinner was served in the middle of the day with tea and supper in the evening.

It was a much-criticised habit of boarding-house keepers to throw strangers together on long tables, so holiday camps consciously sat their customers in small groups. Seats for the whole week were designated on arrival – less than ideal for these teddy boys staying at Corton.

MENU

THURSDAY 24 JULY

BREAKFAST   8 – 9A M
PORRIDGE & MILK
BACON & EGG
FRESH ROLLS
WHITE & BROWN BREAD
BUTTER
PRESERVES · TEA

DINNER   1–2PM
CHICKEN SOUP
ROAST LAMB – MINT SAUCE
GREEN PEAS
POTATOES & BREAD
APRICOT PUDDING
CUSTARD SAUCE
TEA   5 –6PM
GRILLED SAUSAGE
ROAST POTATOES
WHITE & BROWN BREAD
BUTTER
CAKES
PRESERVES
TEA

SUPPER   10 PM
CHEESE
WHITE & BROWN BREAD
COFFEE
PRESERVES CAKES

Specimen Menu.

steam-powered dough mixers, bread slicers, potato peelers, butter spreaders and a specially designed dishwasher capable of cleaning twenty thousand plates after every meal. Technological advances in the 1930s turned holiday camp kitchens into gleaming temples of smooth stainless steel with fixtures and fittings in enamel and chrome. Guests were invited to marvel at the advanced refrigeration facilities as well as the modern designs for cooking equipment powered by gas and electricity. Prestatyn Holiday Camp had a fryer in its kitchen that was reputedly one of the largest in the world, capable of cooking two thousand portions of fish simultaneously. The new Squires Gate kitchen, fitted in 1939, could chip 1,800 pounds of potatoes an hour. In charge of six up-to-date ovens, and refrigerators large enough to store 1,800 pounds of meat and 80 stone of fish, its Belgian chef was likened by one journalist to a mechanic more than a cook. In the days

superbly cooked...

Everything is cooked in our bright, modern, spotlessly clean, well-equipped kitchens. We see that only the best quality food reaches our storerooms! Most of the vegetable and salad stuffs are grown on Maddiesons own allotments, and all perishable foods and dairy products come from local farms— so you know you're getting 'farm fresh meals!

...by experts!

All meals are hygienically prepared under strict supervision. Our chef is one of the finest cookery experts in the country and he knows just how to produce the most appetising dishes to please every Littlestone camper, however hearty his appetite! And for the babies, freshly prepared strained foods are supplied from our own kitchens, but proprietary foods are not supplied.

Clean, well-equipped kitchens were still a selling point in the 1960s and the brochure for Maddieson's Littlestone camp in Kent assured potential customers of 'farm fresh meals' with vegetables and salad grown on the camp allotments.

At Butlin's, hearty British food was plated up and brought into the dining-room in heated trolleys. Waitresses extracted six plates at a time to carry to their tables on a portable plate rack.

before convenience foods and factory farming, meals were based around traditional meat dishes, and by the 1960s a weekly dinner menu at a Pontin's camp would typically feature two roast beef, two roast chicken, one roast pork, one roast lamb and on the last night roast turkey with all the trimmings.

For women, it was not simply the quality of the food but the fact that they did not have to prepare it that was important. Holiday camps targeted housewives in their advertising, offering them a week of freedom from

BUTLIN'S BOGNOR REGIS
A Typical Dining-room

Enjoying the sunshine outside a Warner's chalet. Holidays were a time to put on those fabulous 1950s frocks and forget about cooking and cleaning.

bedmaking, darning socks, hot stoves and washing up. In the 1950s Prestatyn Holiday Camp promised mothers the chance to do things they had not done for years:

> ... a set of tennis with a new found friend; a canter on horseback; lazing and bathing on the beach or the swimming pool; brushing up your dancing

This postcard was sent from Clacton in 1964. A content mother wrote on the back: 'Jacqueline isn't any bother at all, she loves to be in the nursery with the other children. Pauline we see only at meal time...'

BUTLIN'S
Typical Children's Playroom

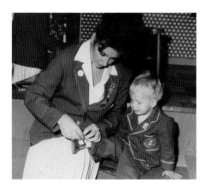

at special free lessons; or simply knitting and gossiping – yes, let's be honest, gossiping whilst you breathe the wonderful sea air and laze in the sunshine.

In a confiding tone, the brochure appealed to wives everywhere: 'We know Dad does his best, bless him; but we've got to make allowances for the fact that he is only a man, after all. He cannot fully appreciate just how you long to drop everything for once ...' This included responsibility for childcare, so the holiday camp obligingly provided free crèche facilities and a team of people to keep the children occupied and out of harm's way. Realising that parents also wanted freedom to enjoy evening entertainments, Billy Butlin instituted the 'night owl' chalet patrol. Nurses on bicycles listened along the chalet lines and tried to soothe away any tears before putting out a call to Mother. In the camp bars 'Baby crying' boards would light up with the chalet number in question, and such priority was given to alerting parents that even celebrity performers were liable to interruptions by the compère.

Before the era of statutory holiday pay, most working parents had found a stay away from home with their children prohibitively expensive. The full implications of altered employment law were not felt until after the Second World War, by which time Britain was experiencing a baby boom. Unlike boarding houses, which were notoriously child-unfriendly, holiday camps were already set up to welcome a new generation of visitors, treating them as important guests in their own right. In 1939 children under twelve could stay at Middleton Tower Holiday Camp for half price, and parents were assured that the outdoor playground, 'Kiddies' Corner' and paddling pool, and the indoor nursery and playroom, were always 'under qualified supervision'. Furthermore, 'At meal times Milk, Milk Puddings and Fruit are always available for children'. Evening tea was served at most holiday camps for those too

Above left: A member of the Butlin's Beaver Club has his shoe buckled by a friendly Redcoat 'Auntie'.

Above right: Billy Butlin started the Beaver Club in 1951. Campers aged three to six joined for a year and were expected to follow the club rules set out on their membership card.

Children who spent their holidays at Warner's holiday camps could become members of the Wagtail Club.

Right: Brother and sister Red Indians are photographed on their way to the fancy dress competition at Duporth Holiday Resort, near St Austell, Cornwall, in summer 1966.

Below: The playground at Butlin's Filey was dubbed a 'Children's Wonderland'. There were big toys, a merry-go-round and giant climbing frame, plus miniature buildings to explore. Behind the timber-framed Wendy House the Toadstool House is just visible.

small to stay up until dinner time. Butlin's nursery nurses cooked three meals a day, which they served to campers under the age of two in rows of high chairs eighty to a hundred long. Older children were entertained by 'Aunties' and 'Uncles', their titles suggesting the idea of an extended holiday family. 'Uncle Mick' Millington entertained thousands of Derbyshire miners at their Skegness camp from 1949 till its closure in the early 1990s and was a favourite at the 'Miner's Minor' children's centre. Every Warner's camp had its own 'Uncle Arthur', who drew children out of their chalets by playing a recorder, while parents were left to sleep in. He took children on walks into the camp's private woodlands for lessons in natural history and in his chalet he sang, told stories, did puppet shows and blew balloons. There were 'kids' clubs', fancy dress parties and numerous special activities for children. At holiday camps the whole family could be occupied in different ways at the same time; it was a blissful release for post-war parents.

Above: Holiday camps always had plenty of indoor, wet-weather activities. This action shot was captured by a proud father in the games room at Butlin's Pwllheli.

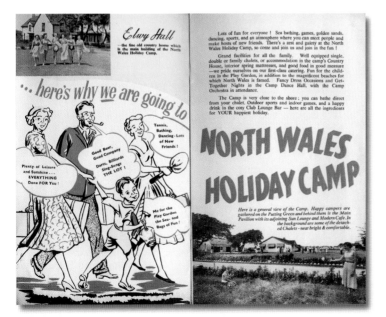

Left: Something for everyone at the North Wales Holiday Camp, near Abergele. This 1950s brochure highlights the range of activities on offer: Father puts 'good beer' first, while his son looks forward to 'bags of fun' by the sea.

ENTERTAINMENTS

H OLIDAY CAMPS tended to be at the seaside because that had become the normal holiday destination. Beaches and sea air were attractions but, as the brochures stressed, there were so many activities and entertainments provided at a holiday camp that guests need never set foot off site. There was always something going on, whatever the time, whatever the weather. Billy Butlin was the master when it came to entertaining thousands of holidaymakers at once, the huge scale of his camps generating a vast budget for celebrity performers, sports instructors, big venues and novelties, which in the 1960s included monorails, chair lifts, a dry ski slope and water-skiing. In addition there were beauty contests, talent shows and sporting challenges in which everyone was invited to take part. These were holiday camp staples, common to them all, however large or small, often organised by volunteer committees that changed every week. It was not just the price that was inclusive – the whole holiday camp ethos encouraged reserved Britons to join in and make new friends.

Unfortunately the first campers who turned up at Butlin's Skegness in 1936 were so unused to the concept of free entertainments that they wandered around the site aimlessly, keeping to their tight-knit family groups. It was soon clear to Billy Butlin that excellent and varied amenities were not enough on their own. Three days into his first season, faced with bored and diffident campers, Butlin asked Norman Bradford, a trusted employee since the 1920s, to liven things up. That night, at the end of his comedy routine, Bradford asked campers to shake hands with the people to their right and then their left. Laughter soon triumphed over reticence and the dining-room buzzed with conversation. A week later, the local outfitters had finished sewing the scarlet blazer, made to Butlin's specifications with a letter 'B' on its breast pocket, and Norman Bradford bounded up on stage in his distinctive new uniform to become the first Redcoat. He was soon joined by colleagues picked for their friendliness, and by 1946 there was one Redcoat for every twenty-five campers. Brokers of social interaction in a crowd, their motto was 'friend, philosopher and guide'. Owing to Butlin's

Opposite:
A big band plays for post-war campers. Every Butlin's had its own resident musicians: in the late 1940s Ronnie Munro and his New Dance Orchestra were at Ayr; Jimmy Masson was the bandleader at Mosney, near Dublin.

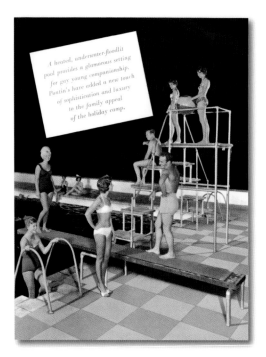

A heated, underwater-floodlit pool provides a glamorous setting for gay young companionship. Pontin's have added a new touch of sophistication and luxury to the family appeal of the holiday camp.

In 1961 underwater-floodlit swimming pools were such an innovation that this picture appeared full-page on the back of the promotional *Pontin News*.

Young and old line up for 'physical jerks' after breakfast at Corton Beach. Holiday camps provided the perfect setting to try out the latest 1930s fitness craze.

canny recognition of promotional possibilities, Redcoats soon became a powerful corporate symbol, later copied by Pontin's and Warner's, who had Bluecoats and Greencoats respectively.

From the outset, sport played a big part in the activities on offer at holiday camps. The young men who visited Cunningham's Edwardian camp formed into teams for football and cricket on the recreation ground, played tennis and stretched their muscles at tug of war. It was no coincidence that thirty years later the rush of holiday camp building coincided with the health and beauty movement's rise to prominence. Keep-fit classes were scheduled daily, with instruction also available in gymnastics, boxing and swimming. During the 1930s lidos appeared across the country and large open-air pools lay at the heart of high-end holiday camp developments, a focus for the new sunbathing craze as well as gala displays and diving. Squires Gate advertised its new 'model' pool in 1939, boasting that the fresh water was aerated by fountains, warmed by gas and changed six times a day. For other outdoor pursuits, equipment such as croquet mallets and golf clubs was free to

Left: An early crazy golf course among 1930s chalets at the South Devon Holiday Camp in pre-Pontin's days.

Centre: Most camps had an outdoor pool but at St Leonards-on-Sea it was absolutely integral; the Bathing Pool Holiday Camp was converted from a huge inter-war lido in the 1960s.

A young swimmer at Pwllheli is captured mid-jump. Butlin had a fondness for hanging plastic parrots and foliage from the ceiling of his indoor pools but by 1974 this decoration was looking decidedly shabby.

hire with a chalet key as deposit. Even horses were provided at some bigger camps, though a charge was usually made to go riding. Indoors, the billiards room was a prerequisite of camp life and on rainy days table tennis proved a popular pastime.

Well into the 1960s, the sporting side of holiday camp life embraced as many silly races as possible. Entrants lined up for the sack race, three-legged race, leap-frog, wheelbarrow race and egg-and-spoon race. To give people an incentive to take part, a competitive component was quickly built in, with campers winning 'house' points on

The first two indoor heated pools were built in 1957 as part of Butlin's twenty-first anniversary investment programme. Glass viewing panels below the water level provided a unique backdrop to neighbouring cafés.

the public-school model. At Caister Holiday Camp the Bears tried to beat the Lions, while the dining-rooms of Warner's camps were divided into Cads and College to 'foster a spirit of friendly rivalry'. Butlin opted for royal names, campers at his largest sites being split into Kent, Gloucester, Windsor and York houses, each with its own dining room.

Every holiday camp had a games room. In 1962 this new 'Pavilion' was built at Gunton Hall in Norfolk, complete with special rooms for television and teenagers. Its modern design was in striking contrast to the original Georgian mansion to its right.

Fibreglass pedalos keep children amused at Pontin's Blackpool in the late 1970s. Boating lakes were one of many amenities transferred from the seafront to the holiday camp. Note the back-to-back chalet terraces behind.

Two days' worth of entertainments as offered by Warner's in the mid-1950s. Sports, music and camp competitions provided a good mixture of activities, with nightly events in the ballroom after high tea.

The same points principle applied to non-athletic contests, with a category for every member of the family. Camp queens were chosen at the beginning of the holiday week, the Derbyshire Miners at Skegness voting for their 'Ideal Holiday Girl' and Butlin's campers choosing a 'Holiday Princess'. In 1938 Mass Observation recorders witnessed a very British defence of the underdog at Blackpool's Squires Gate camp:

A ladies' beauty competition for ladies in bathing costumes got no entries. Man waives bathing-costume rule. Twenty-seven ladies enter after persuasion. One white-haired old lady is first entrant and stands half a minute before anyone else comes forward ... Judged by hand-clap. Old lady who entered first wins hands down.

The ladies on the left look as if they have been practising for the camp's three-legged race; all the other pairs are having difficulty – which, of course, was part of the fun.

A beauty contest at Duporth Holiday Camp in 1947. The girl who attracted the longest line of campers claimed the title of Miss Duporth for the week.

Squires Gate ran a 'Personality Girl' competition in the early 1950s. Winners got free holidays as a prize, a common award that ensured repeat business at holiday camps.

Titles varied but often entailed the elected 'Miss' taking the appropriate camp name. Wearing the sash could ultimately prove a dubious honour as it meant judging the children's competitions and the strong possibility of being thrown into the camp pool. As a variation on a theme, Butlin's campers in the 1950s entered Princess Elizabeth and Marilyn Monroe look-alike competitions. Prestatyn Holiday Camp hosted the 1954 'Great Britain's Esther Williams Competition' sponsored by Pan American Airlines, with a trip to Florida for the lucky winner.

While women competed in the beauty stakes, more or less seriously, their fathers and husbands fought it out for the Ugly Face title or rolled up their long johns in the hope of displaying the camp's most Knobbly Knees. The Little Canada holiday camp on the Isle of Wight capitalised on its name and awarded the unique honour of 'King Mountie'. Bonny Babies were judged on their mother's knee, Grandmothers got the opportunity to be Glamorous, and little girls stood in line for the 'Junior Miss' competition. Their brothers could enter the Butlin's Tarzan contest or, if they preferred not to pose in a pair of trunks, there was the Smartest Boy award for snappy dressers. Sponsorship deals led Butlin's to host such bizarre contests as the Rizla Cigarette Rolling Competition and Shaver of the Week. Challengers for the latter accolade had to shave at the Philishave counter in the camp shop so that their beard

Lining up for the Best Husband competition at Butlin's Brighton Hotel in March 1962. Number Four took first prize; he was on his honeymoon.

Towels and crêpe paper make a good showing in the children's fancy dress competition at Pontin's Camber Sands in 1970. An international dimension is provided by a Cossack and, in the centre, a matador.

shavings could be collected and measured. When it came to fancy dress, everyone was included. Many camps offered costume hire, but making it yourself was half the fun and, alongside the people who adapted whatever was at hand, there were competitors who planned their outfits well ahead.

Whether or not you won a prize, there were sure to be lots of laughs at the fancy dress ball.

Dancing was a popular social activity during the heyday of British holiday camps and was a key constituent of the entertainments package. Couples could dance the night away for free – every night if they chose – while singletons found a ready supply of partners among fellow chalet occupants. Ballrooms tended to be simple buildings that fulfilled the basic requirements of a large open space with a sprung floor, but bigger camps sought to create more opulent surroundings. Butlin claimed his Empress ballrooms gave 'a realistic Viennese setting' and the *East Essex Gazette*, reporting from Clacton, was impressed by 'protruding fairy tale castles as the walls and Tudor pillars supporting a centre balcony ...' In 1957 the Derbyshire Miners' centre at Skegness unveiled its new Sea Breeze Ballroom, decorated in duck-egg blue and gold, with 2,000 square feet of African hardwood on the floor and a mirror ball shimmering from the ceiling. Butlin's was celebrating its twenty-first season that year and campers were assured that 'Each Camp will have three Ballrooms – one for Modern, one for Old-Time and one for Jive – with expert instruction in all three types of dancing'. Accompaniment was supplied by resident musicians under celebrity bandleaders, such as violinist Mantovani, who played a pre-war Butlin's season with his sixteen-piece dance orchestra. After the war big bands were joined by guitar-based pop groups before discos with recorded music took over.

The range of live entertainment was a huge selling point of the Butlin brand, but plenty of holidaymakers preferred the home-grown variety shows of smaller camps, where the chorus girls doubled as waitresses and the

This Art Deco theatre was brought to Skegness from the 1938 Glasgow Empire Exhibition, where Billy Butlin ran the 16-acre amusement park. Many celebrities performed in the two-thousand-seat auditorium before its demolition at the end of the 1990s.

campers' talent show was the highlight of the week. Billy Butlin was sensible enough to retain these elements, and the talent of well-known performers such as Helen Shapiro, Mike Reid, Alvin Stardust and Catherine Zeta-Jones was spotted at his camps. Other would-be stars became Redcoats. Though few actually made it, campers enjoyed cheering for their new friends in the Redcoat Revue. The presence of *bona fide* celebrities on camp also lifted the Butlin holiday out of the ordinary; where else could you watch Laurel and Hardy judge a Knobbly Knees competition? Sunday evening shows by radio stars allowed campers to put a face to a voice and, in the days before television, postcards home brimmed with excitement at the star seen up close and, moreover, seen for free. Confounding the critics who sniffed at populist holiday camp fare, Butlin also engaged the San Carlo Opera Company from Covent Garden for a post-war production of Puccini's *La Bohème* at the Filey concert hall, inviting four hundred distinguished guests to make the journey with him on a luxury Pullman train. The Royal Philharmonic Orchestra played for the opening of Pwllheli camp, Shakespearean plays were performed by the Bristol Old Vic company, and the International Ballet Company also toured Butlin's theatres. From the early 1950s, serious drama was presented at every camp by a resident repertory company performing four to six different one-hour plays a week.

Variety acts also had their place and comedians such as Bruce Forsyth, Frankie Howerd and Benny Hill got youthful experience at Butlin's, where all comics had to abide by the same rules: no blue material and no going over time.

Unfortunately, we cannot see the act these 1950s campers are watching; some look more impressed than others. Perhaps it was hypnosis, a new form of entertainment in the post-war years.

With such a huge captive audience, Butlin could make useful sponsorship deals. This beer mat from around 1960 promotes a popular drink of the time.

The sale of alcohol was hugely profitable, so entertainments were never permitted to hinder people's ability to get to the bar. By the early 1960s Billy Butlin welcomed one million visitors a year and was listed in the *Guinness Book of Records* as the largest beer retailer in the British Isles. Though this could cause problems, one solution for dealing with drunks was to drive them off camp in a van and leave them to make their own way back. From the early days holiday camps got around the licensing laws by being members-only clubs. Every paying guest automatically got membership and, as proof of this, the camp badge was to be worn at all times.

Though they sold a modern holiday experience, camps also took design inspiration from the past, as seen here in Tudor Bar at Middleton Tower, near Morcambe.

Club rooms generally aimed to give the impression of designed spaces even if, in reality, this just meant adding colourfully painted Lloyd Loom chairs. More ambitious themed bars existed from the 1930s onwards, for example the Buccaneers' Cave at Squires Gate, where artificial boulders were

formed into 'romantic grottoes' and special lighting gave the effect of stormy seas under scudding clouds. Sound effects were provided by a wind machine that could simulate the noise of waves crashing on a pebble beach. The mock-Tudor style used by Butlin on his chalets was also employed in bars, where 'the interior decoration resembles a courtyard to a Hertfordshire farm' and drinks were served through fake mullioned windows.

As his camps grew in size, Butlin built simple two-storey steel-framed buildings that allowed for a highly flexible internal layout. If they were architecturally undistinguished on the outside, careful attention was paid to creating colourful bars, games rooms, quiet lounges and cafés on the inside. A Butlin's camp could boast as many as fifteen different bars, each designed to appeal to different audiences and age groups. When an unknown Cliff Richard first played at Clacton's Pig and Whistle Bar in 1958 he was accused of making a racket by customers who preferred a singsong and a good knees-up; his covers of Elvis Presley songs were better received in the South Seas Coffee Bar. In the Crazy Horse, Beachcomber, French, Gaiety and Blinking Owl bars an eclectic mix of murals and models, plastic vegetation, hanging signage and lampshades produced a holiday environment quite unlike the local pub at home. The Derbyshire Miners' Skegness camp also received an exotic touch when the new 'Follow Me Inn' was fitted out with tanks of tropical fish and cactus plants atop the walls. Once in, people had to be

The contemporary club interior at Cornwall's Duporth Holiday Resort in 1965. According to the brochure, residents 'may enjoy the drink of their choice in a happy and pleasant atmosphere'.

persuaded to leave again at closing time, so holiday camps often had a goodnight song to signal when it was time for guests to retire to their chalets.

Accusations of enforced jollity or 'injected whoopee' were made from the beginning but, as *Picture Post* journalist Tom Wintringham perspicaciously observed in 1939, the majority of British seaside promenades were packed with people for the same reason that the new holiday camps were proving popular: 'We want to see and do things, laugh at and with people, be "in" things.' Critics patronisingly suggested that as working men were organised by the factory clock on a daily basis they needed the same coercion to enjoy themselves on holiday. This was unfair, not least because Butlin's, the target of most criticism, drew its clientele from the lower middle classes, catering for clerical rather than shop-floor workers. As John Hudson recalled in his memories of northern wakes week holidays, 'It was rather posh going to Butlin's in the early years. In 1946 you were definitely doing alright if you aspired to a week in your own self-contained chalet ... The only family on our street that managed a week at Prestatyn was headed by a man who sold insurance for the Pru.'

During the war pulling together became a mantra for survival, and this spirit of camaraderie has since been used to explain why people put up with 'Butlinism' after hostilities ceased. Yet those who actually visited the camps

When campers wanted to relax, they could sit in the 'Quiet Lounge' where nothing happened at all. During the war Butlin bought art in job lots. His interest was more in the area each painting would cover than in its subject.

Forming a camp conga was a useful way of emptying the bar. The man just out of shot on the right is definitely getting into the spirit, if his energetic kick is anything to go

discovered that the critics' case had been overstated. Historian J. A. R. Pimlott visited Clacton on a rainy day in 1946 and 'saw little evidence of regimentation or organized "jollying" and heard little of "Radio Butlin". The proportion of campers engaged on anything active was small.' Instead, people were taking the opportunity to relax in an atmosphere of general informality. A packed timetable of activities was published so that people could pick and choose according to their tastes, *not* because they were expected to do everything.

Billy Butlin got the idea for his Beachcomber cabaret bars on a visit to Los Angeles in the late 1950s. Every fifteen minutes lighting and sound effects made the painted volcano erupt. Hawaiian music and grass-skirted staff completed the effect.

Maddieson's mirror

swinging seaside holidays

Showtime at Maddieson's

with loads of fun for all the family

THE VERY BEST HOLIDAY VALUE

mix and make friends at Maddieson's

Maddieson's the friendly camps with do-as-you-please freedom

THE HOLIDAY CAMP PHENOMENON

L OYALTY to the holiday camp concept and to favourite sites and operators was impressively high but it would remain so only as long as camps provided the leisure experience people wanted. In the 1930s, holiday camps were modern and egalitarian. Once the weekly fee was paid, no-one could spend more than anyone else; those wealthy enough to arrive in their own car were no different to people who came by train to the camp station. Everything was free to everyone. Campers bought into a temporary community, which, at Butlin's, had all the amenities of a small town: shops, post-office, hairdressing salons, doctor, even a resident artist. Camp chaplains spent the whole season on site, leading Sunday services and providing a consoling ear at any hour of day or night. Amid this reassuring familiarity, no demand was made of campers beyond their enjoyment.

In 1948 one in twenty British holidaymakers went to Butlin's and another 200,000 would have done so had there been room to accept their bookings. The other chains welcomed their share while thousands more campers chose small family-run sites, often travelling to different areas of the country each year. Even out of season, the camp spirit was quite extraordinary. Friends made among the chalets met again at camp reunions, generally held when the weather was cold and memories of sunny summer days would prompt bookings for the forthcoming season. Pontin's and Butlin's hired the Royal Albert Hall for the national finals of camp competitions, and the Butlin's Beaver Club had its own event to capitalise on childhood pester power. For the rest of the year there were Butlin's social clubs; over the winter of 1946–7 forty of these volunteer-run groups were set up in towns and cities around the country with the assistance of visiting Redcoats.

The 1950s and 1960s were decades of profit and expansion for the market leaders. The generation that was told it had never had it so good went to holiday camps in droves. Butlin's exceeded a million campers a year in 1963 and Pontin's moved away from its 'small unit' image with large new sites in the North-west. At the same time competition from other types of holiday increased. Caravan parks were growing in size and number, many of them

Opposite:
In the mid-1960s Maddieson's had three camps on the Kent coast and one in Norfolk. Friendliness, fun and freedom remained the watchwords, with the added promise of up-to-date 'swinging seaside holidays'.

having the social clubs, bars, swimming pools and entertainments that had been the exclusive province of holiday camps. People at all social levels enjoyed more freedom and, as car ownership rose, fixed mealtimes were losing their appeal. Fred Pontin questioned the basic assumption that holiday camps should provide an all-inclusive package and introduced his self-catering 'Rent-a-Chalet' idea at Wick Ferry, near Christchurch, before rolling it out at other sites. He also built new brick accommodation blocks with fitted kitchens and upgraded older chalets to include *en suite* bathrooms and toilets. In his dining-rooms Pontin dispensed with waitresses and let campers serve themselves when they were ready; his 'tray-and-away' system offered such novelties as salad bars and carousels stacked with different dessert choices. By meeting changing expectations in this way, the company enjoyed a boom into the 1970s.

By 1960 the Butlin's reunion was spread over four days at the Albert Hall with music, celebrity appearances, camp contest grand finals and the National Veleta Dance Trophy.

Everyone say 'cheese'. Campers in fancy dress pose for a group photograph in the late 1950s. People willingly took part because community spirit was among the chief attractions of holidaying at a camp.

Left: The brochure for 1972 set out Pontin's holiday options at home and abroad. The 'Rent-a-Chalet' idea was well in tune with popular demand; self-catering accounted for 43 per cent of all holidays that year, compared to just 12 per cent in 1951.

An aerial view of Pontin's Southport, which was built from scratch in 1968 at a cost of £2.5 million. On the circular site there was accommodation for four thousand, an Olympic-size swimming pool, a massive ballroom and a supermarket for self-catering residents.

Butlin's was forced to follow suit after recording its first ever loss in 1965. Two years later bed and breakfast holidays were available and under the auspices of Bobby Butlin, Billy's son and successor, the firm began building self-contained three-room flats. Prestatyn Holiday Camp introduced caravans and its self-catering flats were in great demand, employees noting in 1967 that 'the cloth cap, at one time a regular visitor, is vanishing'.

In its place came a new force in society – the teenager. Groups of single boys and girls found freedom from adult supervision at holiday camps; there was plenty to do and, just as importantly, plenty of other teenagers to do it with. During the summer months there could be three thousand young people at a time at a single Butlin's, making use of the rock 'n' roll ballrooms, jukeboxes and coffee bars. Special single-sex chalets were fitted out with double bunk beds to sleep four, with a 10s reduction for sharing. Catering for this affluent new market, however, was not without its problems. Separate sections of the dining-room to keep food fights away from visiting families were one thing, but gang trouble and vandalism also became an increasing issue. Security patrols along the chalet lines did not prevent all-night parties, and evidence that the sexual revolution had come to Butlin's only served to put off core campers further. The company stopped taking bookings from groups of single teenagers in 1968.

Competition from abroad led the big holiday camp operators to undertake foreign ventures – with varying degrees of success. Both Butlin and

The sombrero became a symbol of Spanish package holidays and gave its name to the café at Hayling Island's Sunshine Holiday Camp. Against foreign competition, the camp offered 'all the colour, fun and romance of the Continent, only 70 miles from London'.

Teenage boys and girls swap clothes for 'Topsey-Turvey' night at Pontin's Osmington Bay in the late 1960s. Holiday camps gave many young people their first taste of adult freedom.

Pontin built Irish camps immediately after the Second World War, at Mosney and Trabolgan respectively, to take advantage of Ireland's lack of rationing. Riding high, Butlin then set out to transplant his winning formula to the Bahamas. His attempt to give Redcoats to the Americans proved a financial disaster that almost lost him his job and his company. Pontin had greater success in the 1960s because his European investments were predicated upon the idea of giving his existing customers the holiday camp entertainment they loved, with cheap alcohol and guaranteed sunshine. The first 'Pontinental' resort opened at Pineta Beach, Sardinia, in 1963.

Potters Residential Holiday Club

By the 1970s there was a general move away from the old holiday 'camp' name. Potter's at Hopton-on-Sea has been owned by the same family for three generations and is now the United Kingdom's only 'five-star' holiday 'village'.

At Cayton Bay, near Scarborough, Wallis's camp converted to self-catering and adopted the American 'motel' name. Pride in this development led to internal floor plans featuring on their postcards.

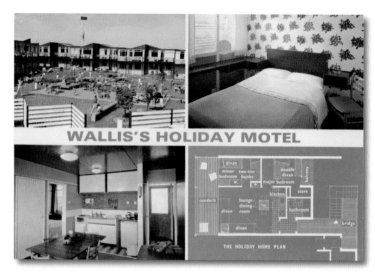

WALLIS'S HOLIDAY MOTEL

A little cowgirl takes centre stage by the pool at NALGO's Croyde Bay centre in the early 1980s. Children have always been well looked after at holiday camps.

Others followed in Majorca, Ibiza and Torremolinos. Every apartment had its own bathroom and tea-making machine; the restaurants served plain English food, with one Mediterranean option for brave souls. Thanks to cheap charter flights, Pontin could offer two reasonably priced weeks on the Mediterranean when foreign package holidays were still a novelty.

The hugely popular BBC television series *Hi-de-Hi*, first aired in 1980, was an indication of the place holiday camps had secured in the British consciousness. But it was no coincidence that the affectionately drawn characters staffing the fictional Maplin's camp did so in 1950s costume. It might have been seen as a compliment had it not implied that holiday camps were stuck in the past. This was already a challenging period. Butlin's had been sold to Rank in 1972; the camps were looking their age and the thousands of peak bookings required to meet the high labour and running costs of such huge sites were no longer assured. In 1983 Clacton and Filey camps were closed. Pontin's was bought by Coral in 1978 and Warner's by Grand Metropolitan in 1983 before a Rank takeover five years later. Smaller sites exchanged their chalets for static caravans, having already dropped the 'holiday camp' label. Revamps and re-brandings as 'holiday centres', 'villages' and 'parks' sought to address the image problem. Then, in the late 1980s, a new competitor entered the market from Holland: Center Parcs lured middle-class guests to villas set in natural woodland. Their slogan, 'We wouldn't dream of organising you', was a clear dig at the old holiday camps. Considered deeply unfashionable, the famous Butlin's brand disappeared as sites were given individual names like Somerwest World for Minehead and Starcoast World for Pwllheli. It is now back, minus the apostrophe, with a serious programme of investment at the three remaining sites – Skegness, Bognor

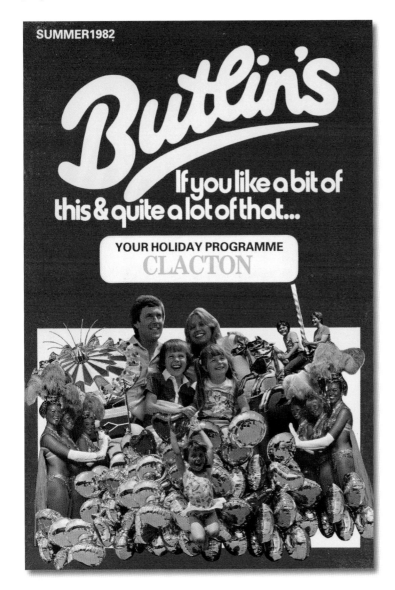

A programme for Butlin's Clacton from summer 1982. To fund improvement work, the Rank Organisation decided to streamline the brand, closing Clacton and Filey camps in the following year.

At the beginning of the twenty-first century Butlins is returning to its roots, providing affordable luxury. Bognor Regis still has old-fashioned carousels but it also has a brand-new Ocean Hotel with disco lifts, a spa and a snow cave.

Regis and Minehead. Pontin's and Warner's also remain significant players in the domestic tourism industry, the latter specialising in adults-only accommodation.

In the mid-twentieth century British holiday camps offered something genuinely different to a population learning to enjoy new leisure opportunities. Yet today there are virtually no architectural remnants of the camps built in the 1930s with such promises of mass-market modernity. Just one 'Elizabethan' chalet survives at Butlins Skegness as a Grade II listed building. The holiday camp's all-inclusive ethos belongs to a specific historic moment, but the recollections of chalets, first kisses, dressing up and winning competitions will last much longer.

DON'T FORGET

to return your chalet key to the office and claim your deposit.

Just a little reminder before you leave...

FURTHER READING

Akhtar, Miriam, and Humphries, Steve. *Some Liked It Hot: The British on Holiday at Home and Abroad.* Virgin Publishing, 2000.

Braggs, Steven, and Harris, Diane. *Sun, Sea and Sand: The Great British Seaside Holiday.* Tempus, 2006.

Butlin, Sir Billy. *The Billy Butlin Story: A Showman to the End.* Robson Books, 1982.

Daniels, Sarah Jane. *Remember Filey Butlins.* East Riding of Yorkshire Council, 2006.

Drower, Jill. *Good Clean Fun: The Story of Britain's First Holiday Camp.* Arcadia Books, 1982.

Ferry, Kathryn. *The British Seaside Holiday.* Shire, 2009.

Gration, Geoff. *The Best Summer of Our Lives: Derbyshire Miners' Holiday Camp.* Breedon Books, 2000.

Hudson, John. *Wakes Week: Memories of Mill Town Holidays.* Alan Sutton, 1992.

Parr, Martin. *Our True Intent Is All for Your Delight: The John Hinde Butlin's Photographs.* Chris Boot, 2002.

Read, Sue. *Hello Campers! Celebrating 50 Years of Butlins.* Bantam Press, 1986.

Ward, Colin, and Hardy, Dennis. *Goodnight Campers! The History of the British Holiday Camp.* Mansell Publishing Ltd, 1986.

Willsher, Peter. *Fred Pontin: The Man and His Business.* St David's Press, 2003.

Wood, Bertha. *Fresh Air and Fun: The Story of a Blackpool Holiday Camp.* Palatine Books, 2005.

WEBSITES
www.butlinsmemories.com
www.postcardnostalgia.co.uk
www.ukholidaycamps.co.uk
www.seasidehistory.co.uk/camps.html

Competing for the title of Holiday Princess at Butlin's Pwhlelli in June 1958.

INDEX